# - *More* -
# Minstrel Ban

Frank Converse's *Banjo Instructor, Without a M*
Performance Notes and Transcriptions
by JOSEPH WEIDLICH

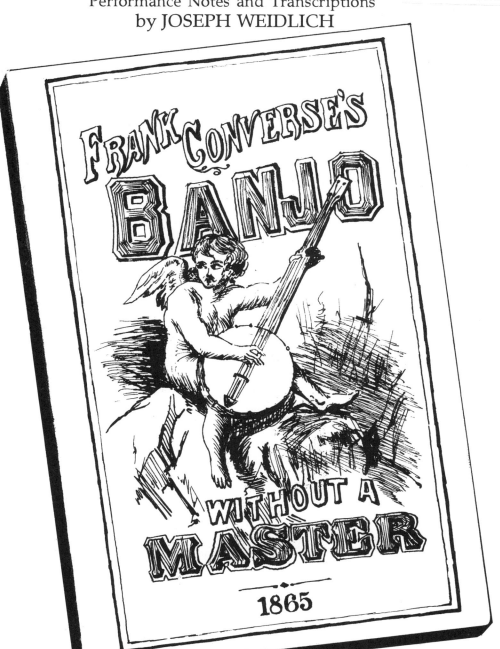

Same size copy of Frank Converse's *Banjo Instructor, Without a Master* (published in 1865 by Dick & Fitzgerald, New York) contains a choice collection of banjo solos, jigs, songs, reels, walk arounds, progressively arranged and plainly explained.

Cover art - The Banjo Lesson (1893) - by Henry Ossawa Tanner
Coursty of Hampton University Museum - Hampton, Virginia

ISBN 1-57424-075-7
SAN 683-8022

Copyright © 1999 CENTERSTREAM Publishing
P.O. Box 17878 - Anaheim Hills, CA 92807

# TABLE OF CONTENTS

\* These songs are available on cassette tape.  See page 48 for details.

*Frank B. Converse*

Frank B. Converse was born in Westfield, Massachusetts in 1837. He was one of the most well-known players and instructors of the banjo by the late 1850's.

# Biography

Joseph Weidlich began his formal musical studies on the classical guitar. He moved to Washington, D.C. in 1972, from his native St. Louis, to teach classic guitar. He performed in several classic guitar master classes conducted by notable students of Andres Segovia (i.e., Sr. Jose Tomas [Spain], Oscar Ghiglia [Italy] and Michael Lorimer [U.S.]).

In 1978, he completed research on and writing of an article on *Battuto Performance Practice in Early Italian Guitar Music (1606-1637)*, for the Journal of the Lute Society of America, 1978 (Volume XI). This article outlines the various strumming practices, with numerous examples, found in early methods published in Italy and Spain in the early 17th century. In the late 1970s he published a series of renaissance lute transcriptions for classic guitar, published by Decamera Publishing Company, Washington, D.C., Which were distributed by G. Schirmer, New York/London.

Joe has two new publications through Centerstream Publishing (distributed by Hal Leonard Corp.) *Minstrel Banjo*--the Briggs' Banjo Instructor from 1855, and *Virginia Reels* -for guitar by George P. Knauff published in 1839. With a new one to shortly be released entitled *The Early Minstrel Banjo, Its Technique and Repertoire*.

The banjo has been no stranger in Joe's musical life. He began learning folk styles in the early 1960s during the folk music boom, later playing plectrum and classic banjo styles. His current research in minstrel banjo demonstrates how that style formed the foundation of clawhammer banjo performance practices.

Most recently he has collaborated with banjo builder Mike Ramsey of Appomattox, Virginia, in designing two prototype minstrel banjos based on the dimensions described in Phil Rice's *Correct Method* [1858] as well as similar instruments made by William Boucher in Baltimore in the 1840s.

# PREFACE

This is the second book in a 3-part series of intabulations of music for the minstrel [Civil War-era] banjo. This particular book of banjo music comes from Frank Converse's *Banjo Instructor, Without a Master* (published in New York by Dick & Fitzgerald), the first of two methods published under his name in 1865 (the other was his *New and Complete Method for the Banjo With or Without A Master*, published by S.T. Gordon [New York]). These were also the first banjo instruction books to appear since 1860, just prior to the beginning of the Civil War. Banjo methods published previously to Converse's were:

> The Complete Preceptor for the Banjo [1851]
> Gumbo Chaff [aka Elias Howe]

> Briggs' Banjo Instructor [1855]
> Thomas Briggs

> Howe's New American Banjo School [1857] [abridged ed., 1859]
> Elias Howe

> Correct Method for the Banjo [1858]
> Phil Rice

> Buckley's New Banjo Book [1860] [?]
> James Buckley

These two books by Converse, when looked at together, straddle the original style of minstrel banjo style (use of right hand thumb and index finger only), which had become popular by the early 1840s, and the development of "elevated" salon music executed on the banjo using guitar style techniques (i.e., using the middle finger for notes on the first string, the index finger for notes on the second string, and the thumb for notes on the third, fourth and fifth strings).[1] In his preface Converse makes it clear that the banjo should hold a prominent position as a musical instrument, but that there was a lack of qualified professors to teach proper music theory and its application in playing the banjo.

*Banjo Instructor, Without A Master*, containing "a choice collection of banjo solos, jigs, songs, reels, walk arounds, etc., progressively arranged, and plainly explained; enabling the learner to become a proficient banjoist without the aid of a teacher," is designed for the beginning student to learn the fundamentals of how to play the banjo "correctly." Thorough measure-by-measure explanations are provided for each of the songs, all of which can be characterized as coming from the traditional minstrel repertoire. Converse's *New and Complete Method for the Banjo With or Without A Master* was designed for the serious musical dilettante, as the repertoire, in addition to containing some traditional minstrel selections in embellished arrangements, introduces a dozen songs in the "guitar" style, plus the first use of key centers other than the use of C and G major[2].

---

[1] For detailed information summarizing the idiomatic playing techniques of the first generation of minstrel banjoists please see my book entitled "The Early Minstrel Banjo: Its Technique and Repertoire."

[2] Prior to this time the usual procedure was to retune the banjo itself to the key center required. In this way the function of the fifth string as either the fifth of C or the octave of G was retained. Converse's experimentation with key signatures used the fifth string as a scaler note other than these two primary functions. The principal minstrel banjo keys used from the mid-19th century to circa 1900 were that of A and E, which correspond to contemporary key centers of C and G respectively.

Converse covers the elements of music, the manner of stringing the banjo, tuning ("If the instrument is in tune, the first three strings sounded open, and in the following order, thus: 3rd, 2nd, 1st, 1st, will commence the air of "Oh Susanna."), etc. The banjo he refers to in his method is fretless as he describes measuring a set distance from the nut to the bridge to tune an individual string (e.g., "Measure the distance from the nut to the bridge, and at one third the distance [measuring from the nut] stop the 4th string with the second finger of the left hand, making E. Tune the 3rd string in unison with it." This information on playing unison notes could be used to play such notes (e.g., open first string at third mark/fret on second string) other than in "natural" open position. A diagram showing the position of the notes on the staff and fingerboard in this method does not indicate use of unison notes on inside strings (which does occur on rare occasions up to this time, but not in this method).

On holding the banjo he advises to sit erect and rest the banjo on the front of the right thigh, "the neck elevated and resting in the left hand between the thumb and forefinger. Rest the right fore-arm on the rim of the instrument near the tail piece, bringing the wrist over the bridge." Regarding using the right hand, he recommends to "partly close the hand, allowing the first finger to project a little in advance of the others. Hold the fingers firm in this position. Slightly curve the thumb. Strike the strings with the first finger (nail) and pull with the thumb."

Staff notation signs for right hand fingering indicates the usual markings for thumb (x) and first finger (1) [I indicate this by a "." as it is the more familiar usage]. He also states that a wavy line placed under a triplet or any collection of notes denotes that you must play them by sliding the first finger across the required strings.

Not to be confused with conventional minstrel fingerboard positions (i.e., the 1st [frets 1-4] and 2nd [frets 5-10], Converse lists five principal positions which are, in reality, chord positions. The <u>first</u> position is a C-chord; the <u>second</u> is an F chord; the <u>third</u> is a barre chord at the fifth fret/mark (an F chord); the <u>fourth</u> is a seventh fret barre for the G chord; the <u>fifth</u> is an natural position F-chord formation which, at the eighth mark/fret (but with an open bass note), is a C chord. Converse uses only the first two of these positions in this method.

## Figure 1

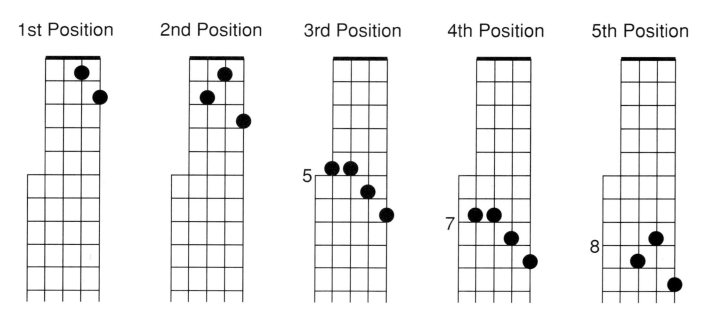

1st Position    2nd Position    3rd Position    4th Position    5th Position

6

With the introduction of frets -- metal or flush -- on the banjo fingerboard, ca. 1860, standard fingerboard position by location of the left hand index finger also begins to appear in banjo methods.

# Compound Meter

Up to this time, only a few songs appearing in banjo methods are in triple meter, i.e., 3/8 or 6/8 time. Of the 30 songs in this method 4 are in triple meter.

# Right Hand Fingerings

When Converse was 18 years old, he was fortunate to be represented in Rice's *Correct Method* as an arranger for four songs and credited as a composer for one song. While Converse occasionally uses established minstrel right hand fingerings (e.g., Cotton Pod Walk Around and Coon Hunt Walk Around), the right hand finger structure which he uses in his *Banjo Instructor*, and develops over the years, was probably influenced by the wide variety of right hand fingerings found in Rice. Following are some examples from Rice:

## Figure 2

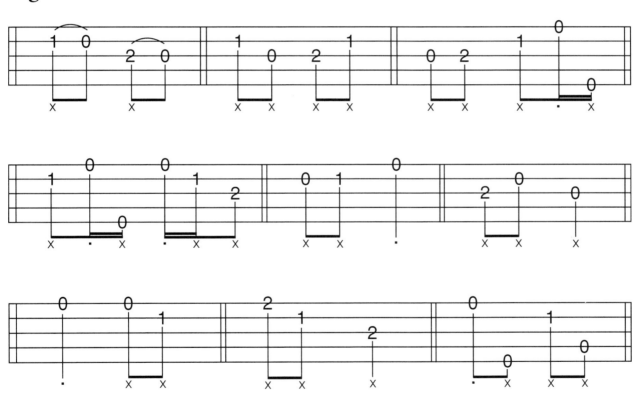

While Converse uses traditional right hand fingerings, the right hand thumb is used much more frequently in his methods than in earlier banjo books.  In the first minstrel banjo methods the index finger would often be used for many of the notes, particularly for notes found on the second string and third strings.  Examination of his arrangements leads me to believe that he used the index finger to play the highest note of a musical phrase, the thumb to play the notes leading up to that note.  The thumb is then dominantly used on the descending notes of the phrase (a more "natural" physiological usage).  Converse always uses the index finger to play notes on the first string, never the thumb.

## Figure 3

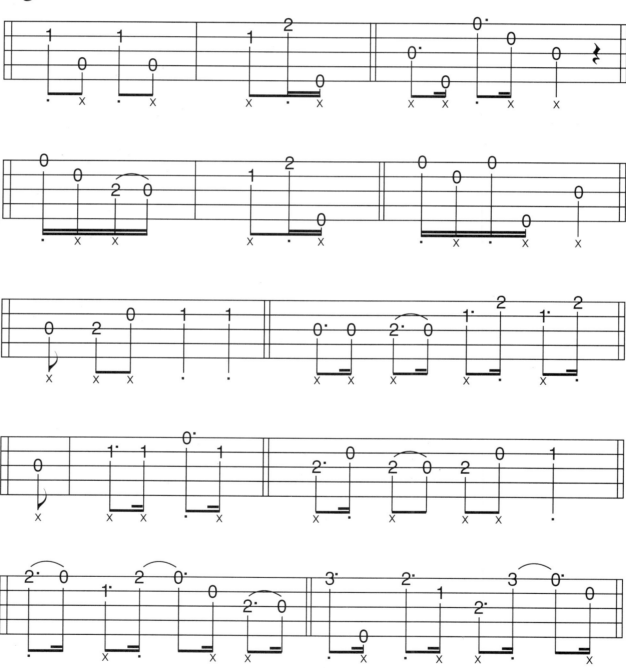

Extended thumb usage is also a result of thumb preparation at the same time that the index finger is executing a note. This procedure can be found throughout Rice's *Correct Method* as well.

## Figure 4

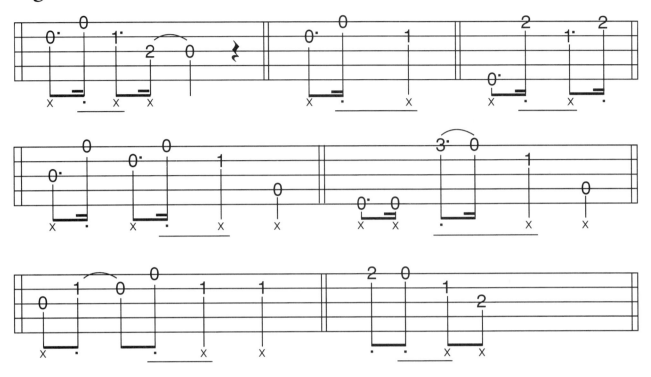

# <u>Slides</u>

The concept of a finger slide is mentioned by Converse. However, this is not a true slide where the initial note is attacked and the arrival note is achieved by the pressure of the finger "sliding" to that note. What he is actually describing is the *portamento*, in which, after the initial note is played, the finger gracefully slides up to the next note and then is played by a new finger attack. In this method, these "slides" always occur on the fourth string with the left hand second finger involved in the execution of the slide. However, in his *New and Complete Method* Converse does on very rare occasions actually use a single attack slide.

We know that this is the correct usage because he explains its execution in his measure-for-measure instructions. For instance, "Place the fourth finger on the 4th string at D..., sound, and then place the second finger on the 4th string at C#; slide back with the second finger to B, sound it; open strings, play 4th":

## Figure 5   Butler's Jig, measure 6

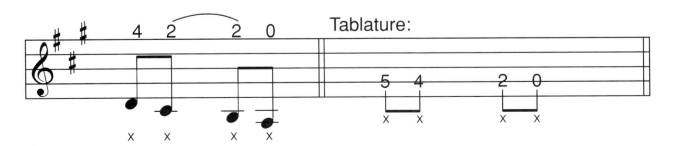

# Slurs

Converse demonstrates a fondness for using a combination descending slur of C to B on the second string and A to G on the third string. This figure is found in various rhythmic guises:

## Figure 6

**Basic Form:**

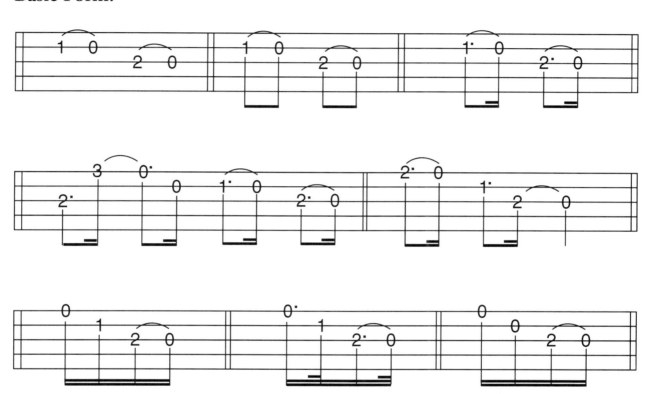

Converse frequently uses descending slurs on off beats,
often using them across bar lines.

## Figure 7

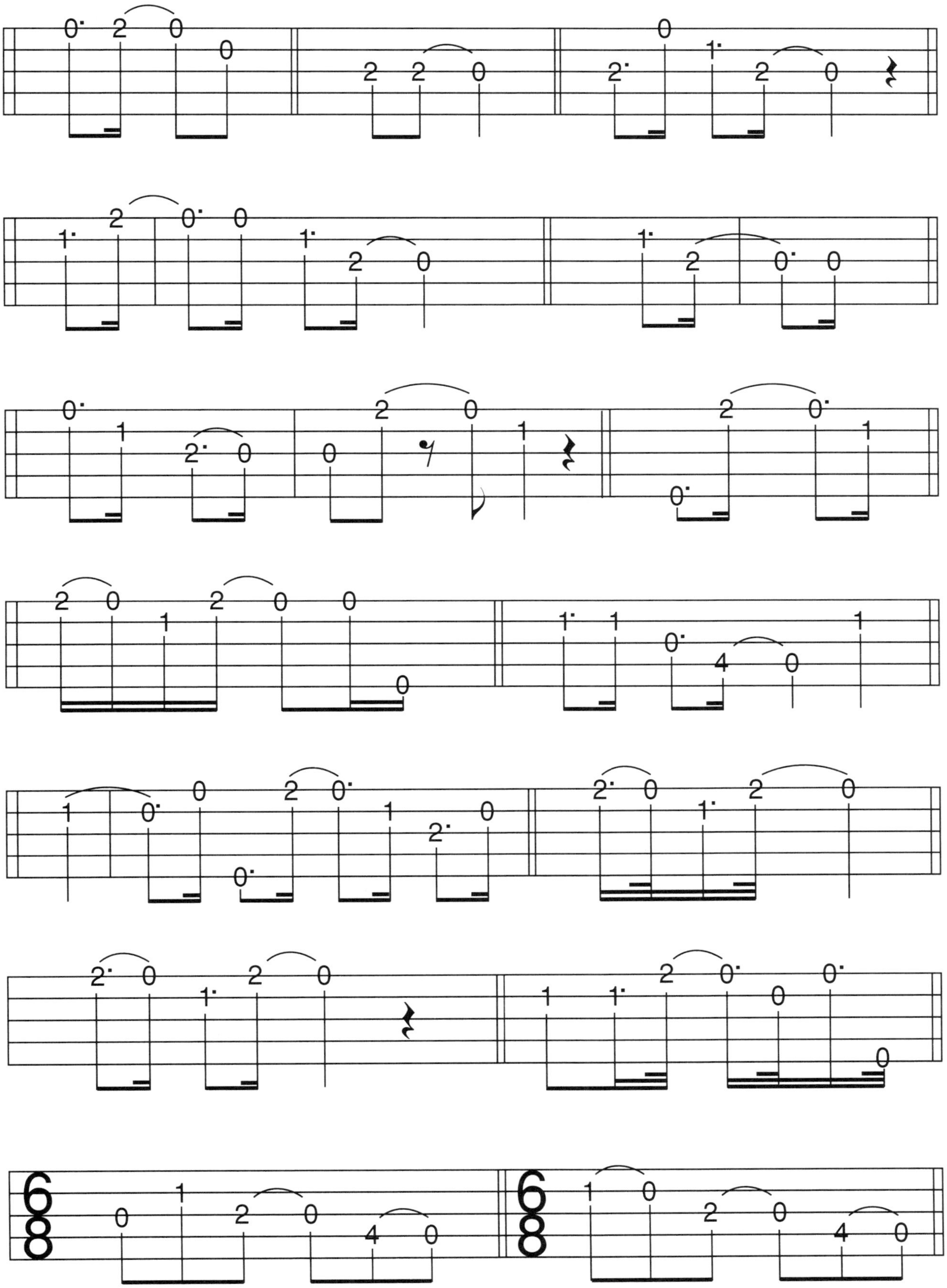

Converse seems to be the first to notate the use of a double descending slur, i.e., one attack on the initial note followed by two additionally slurred notes. He uses it once in his *Banjo Instructor* in the song <u>Arkansas Traveler</u>. In his *New and Complete Method* this slur figure is frequently found, in various rhythmic guises, as are other unique uses of descending slur patterns.

## Figure 8

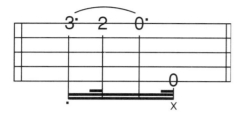

Open string pull-offs first appear in Rice's method. Converse uses it frequently, notated with the left hand finger to be used inside an inverted half circle, ⌣. In this edition, I notate it as a half circle enclosing the tablature number. The second finger is usually used to execute this figure.

## Figure 9

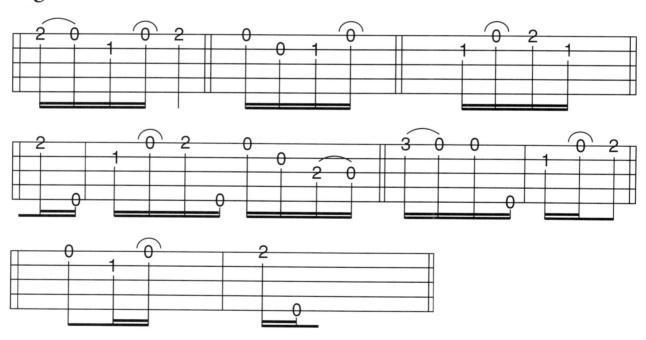

Converse occasionally reverses traditional note sequences:

## Figure 10

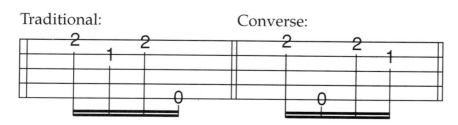

12

# Unusual Right Hand Fingerings

## Figure 11

Converse:                          Traditional:

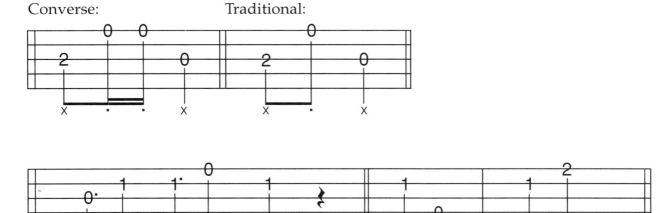

Instances can be found throughout the minstrel banjo literature with repeated notes on the fifth string. The usual practice, when notes on the fifth string are repeated, is to alternate pairs, the fifth string used to play the weak beat (second of the pair). Dotted eighth note pairs of fifth string notes are usually played on the fifth string.

## Figure 12

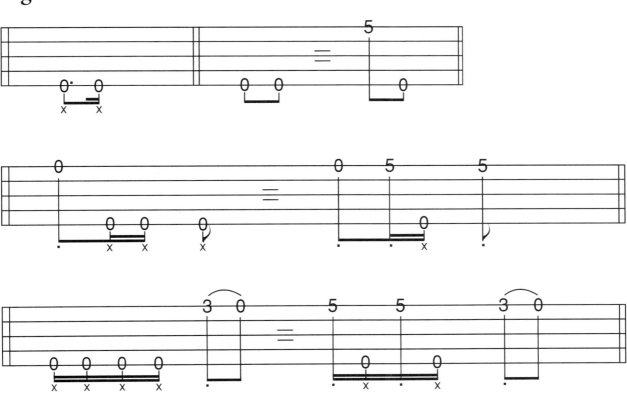

# Fifth String Inversion Notes

Expected placement of fifth string notes is occasionally lowered one octave.

## Figure 13

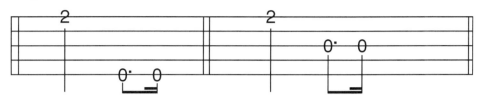

# Eighth Note Rest Usage as a Tied Note

Tied notes are not used in the early banjo methods. Usually rests are used with the understanding/interpretation that the note before the rest is held over to the next sounded note.

**Figure 14**  Luke West's Walk Around [Measures 1-2]. Converse states, "Make the beat on the chords, the chords sounded between the beats."

**Figure 15**  Union Cockade

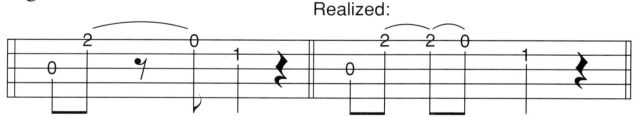

# Barre

Converse uses a unique application of a barre in two songs where the second finger is used to barre only the third and fourth strings.

## Figure 16

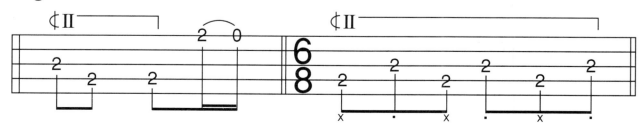

# Nail Glide Examples

**Figure 17**

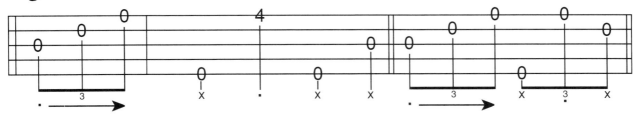

# First/Second Endings

Converse does not provide first/second endings in this collection of songs. Some sections are eight measures long, some four measures long indicating that a repeat is required; sometimes there is a 16-measure section indicating that the first ending and repeat of the section with a second ending is included. Adjustments will have to be made as needed so that the section lengths are uniform, i.e., usually 8 measures long before the repeat.

Whenever there is a pick up note (usually at the beginning of song) a rhythmic modification will have to be made at the end of that section (first ending) so that a return to the beginning can be made, then using the final measure of that section as the second ending.

# NOTES ON THE TABLATURE

In order to reach a wider audience, I have used standard banjo tablature over modern staff notation, even though modern staff notation is used in the minstrel banjo methods. The contemporary banjo tuning of gCGBD should be used [except where notated to raise the fourth string one whole note, from C to D]. This interval structure is the same as the minstrel banjo tuning of eAEG#B used by Converse. The top line of the staff represents the first string, the bottom line the fifth string. Rhythm markings conform to standard usage.

In this edition, I have used an "x" in the tablature to indicate use of right hand thumb and "." to indicate first finger usage.

I have notated nail glide strokes by an arrow: •⟶

# SONGLIST

Juba
Calabash Dance
Cane Brake Reel
Original Essence of Old Virginny
Oh Susanna
Yankee Doodle
Cotton Pod Walk Around
Rattlesnake Jig or Hoop De Dooden Doo
Coon Hunt Walk Around
It Will Never Do To Gib It Up So
Boatman's Dance (The)
Bee Gum Reel
Matt Peel's Walk Around
Rumsey's Jig
Luke West's Walk Around
Bully For You
Walk Into The Parlor
Boston Jig
Butler's Jig
Hyde's Favorite
Union Cockade
Callowhill Jig
My Love Is But A Lassie
Lanagan's Ball
O'Flarharty's Wake
Whole Hog Or None
Charcoal Man (The)
Operatic Jig
Brighton Jig
Arkansas Traveler

**The Ethiopian Serenades on tour in England in 1846. Their performance of a 'Railroad Overture' was said to have caused an 'explosion of laughter'.**

# JUBA
## [Three Varieties]

Converse presents "three varieties" -- really phrases -- which constitute the very popular song/dance Juba. I have followed it with a realized version which comes from his *New and Complete Method for the Banjo With or Without A Master*, published by S.T. Gordon [New York].

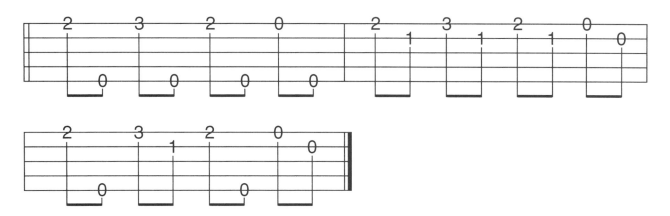

**Cover of "Old Kentucky Home" sheet music**

# Juba (Realized)

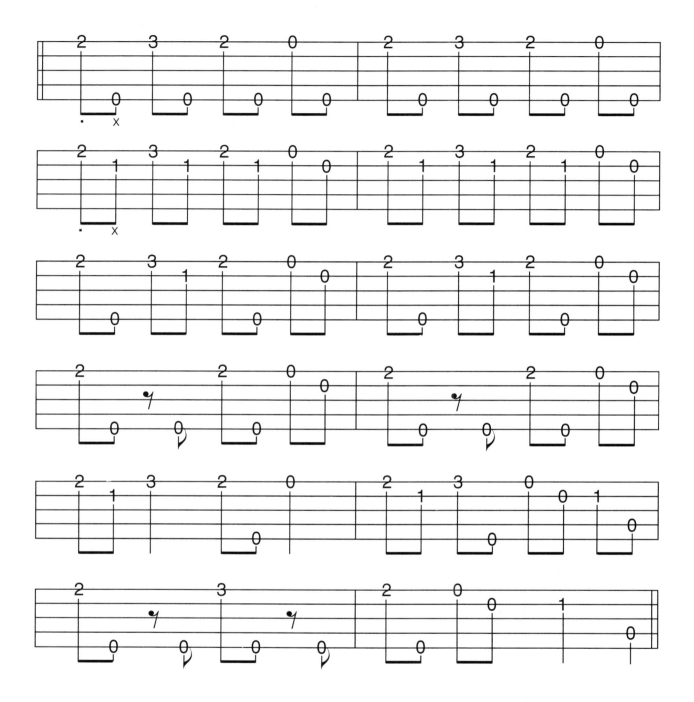

# Calabash Dance

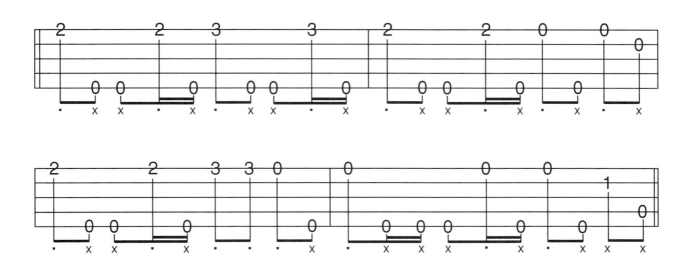

# Cane Brake Reel

The"Rawhide Band",
Pearce Arizona
Turn of the Century
Minstrel Band

# Original Essence of Old Virginny

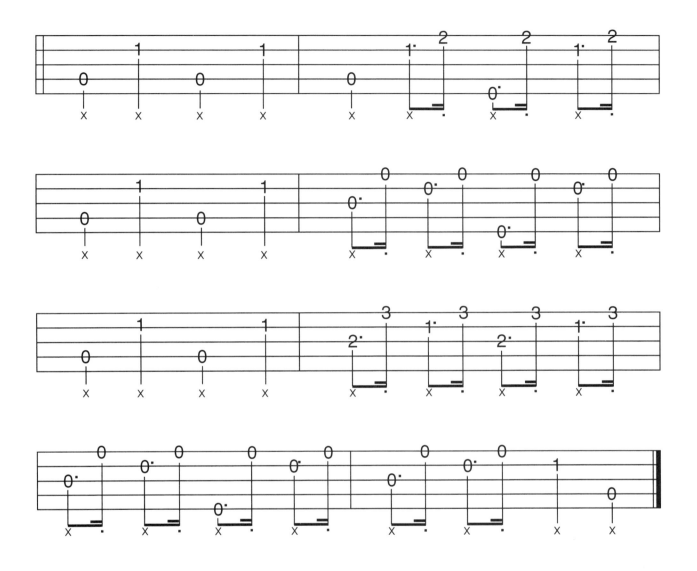

# Oh Susanna

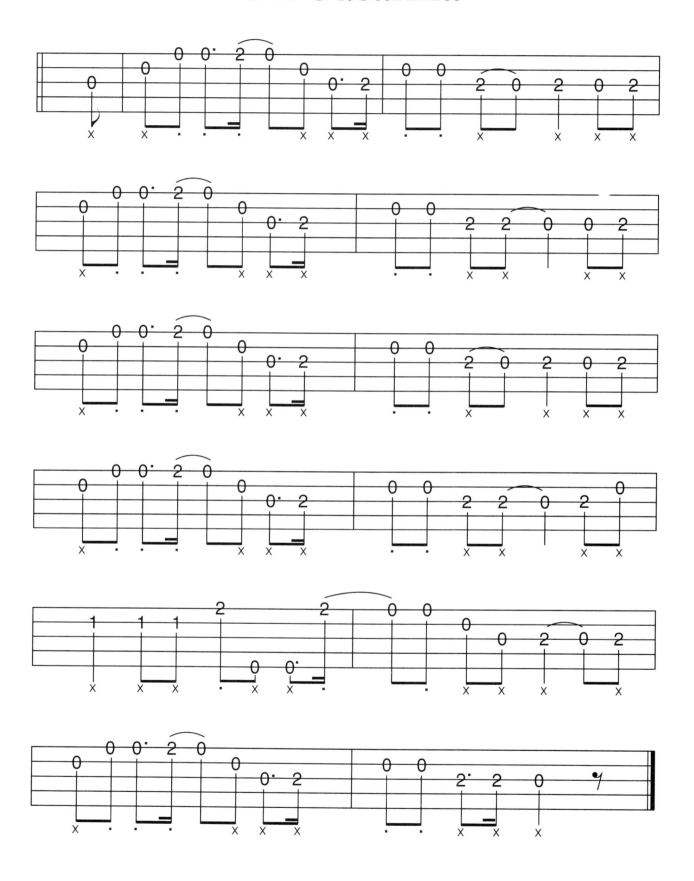

# Yankee Doodle

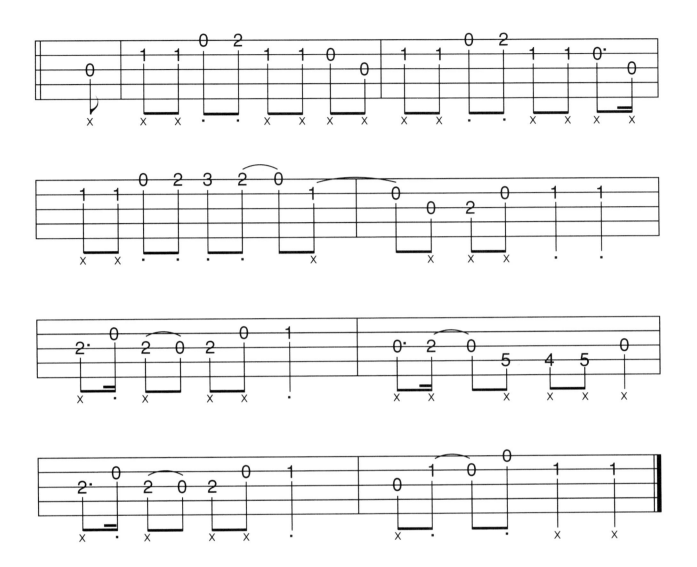

# Cotton Pod Walk Around

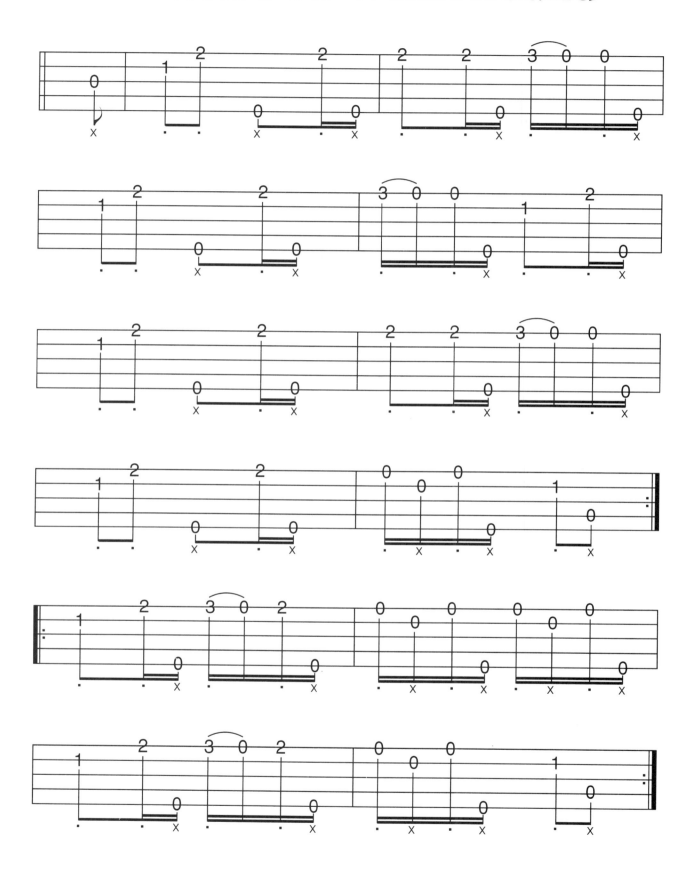

# Rattlesnake Jig
## Or Hoop De Dooden Doo

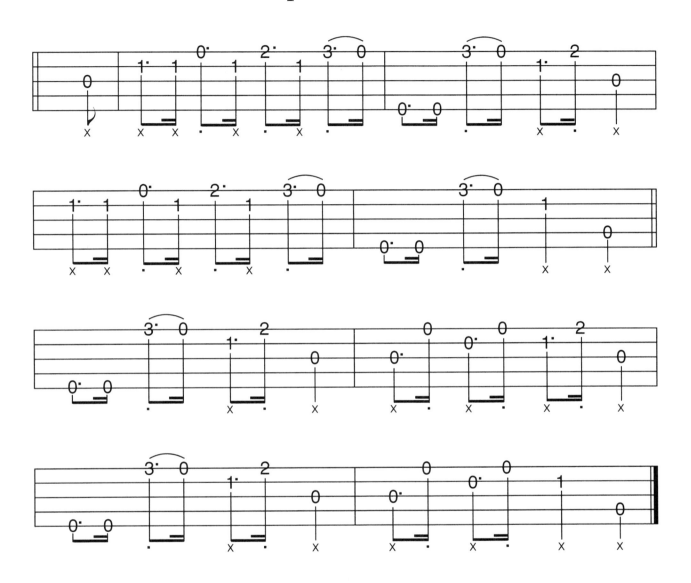

# Coon Hunt Walk Around

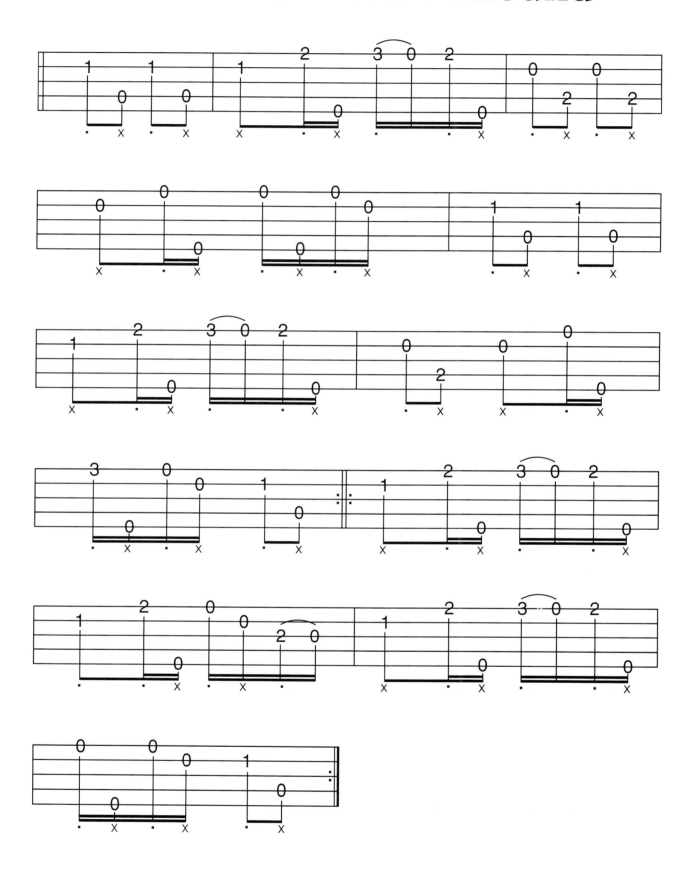

# It Will Never Do To
# Gib It Up So

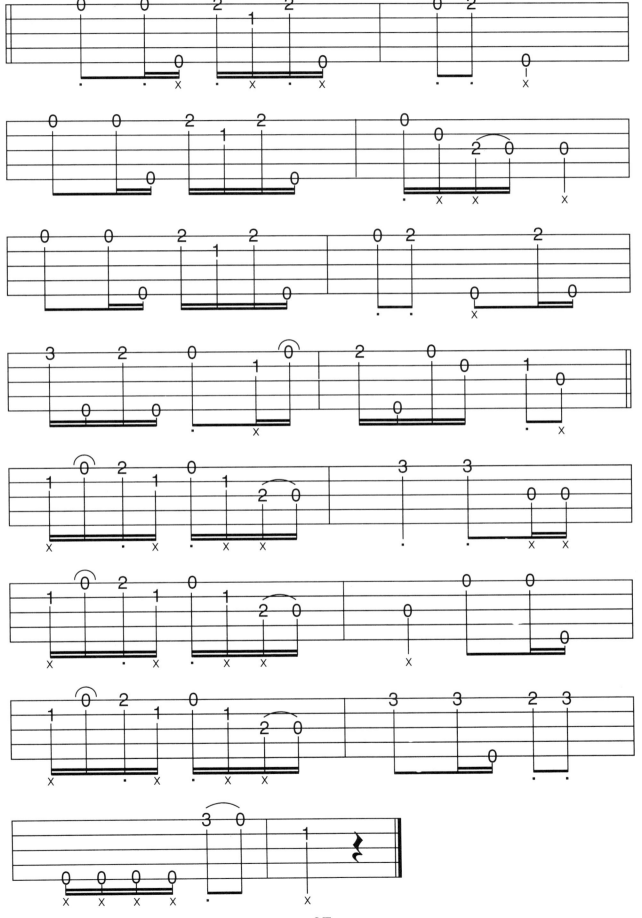

# Boatman's Dance (The)

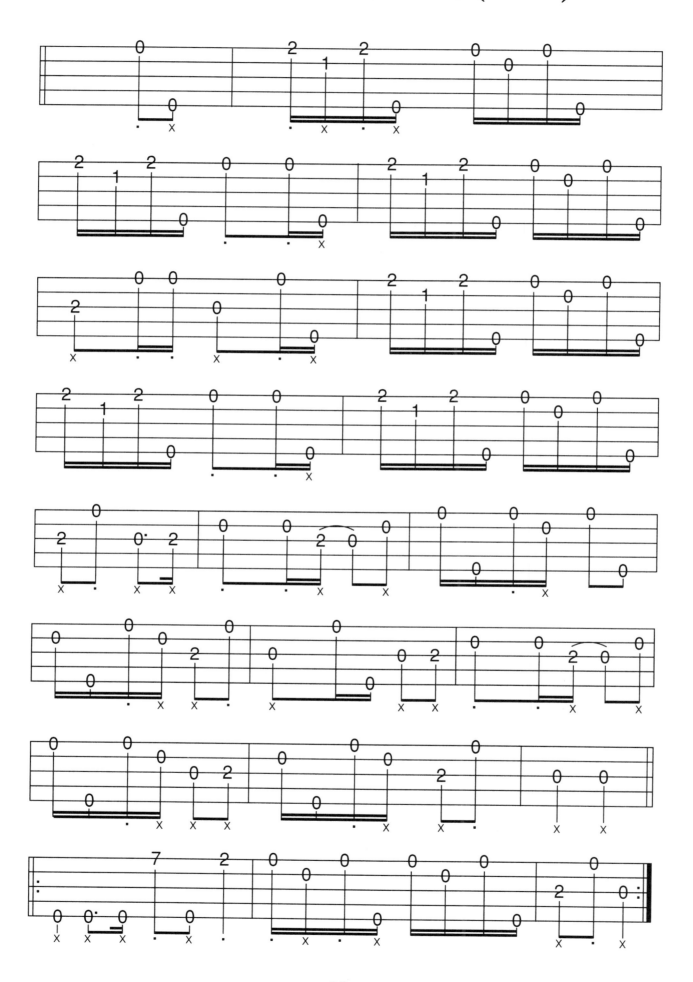

# Bee Gum Reel

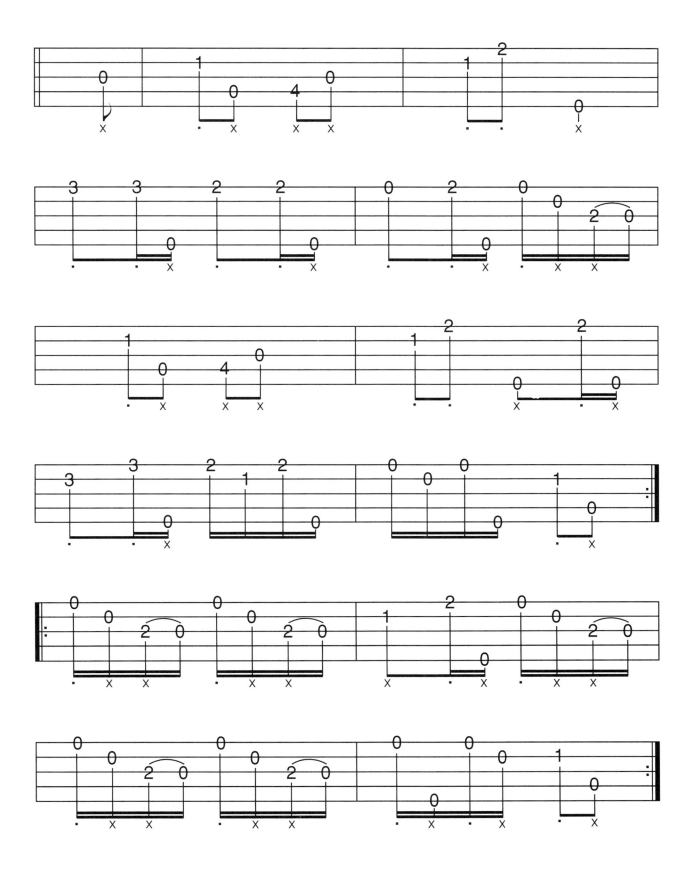

# Matt Peel's Walk Around

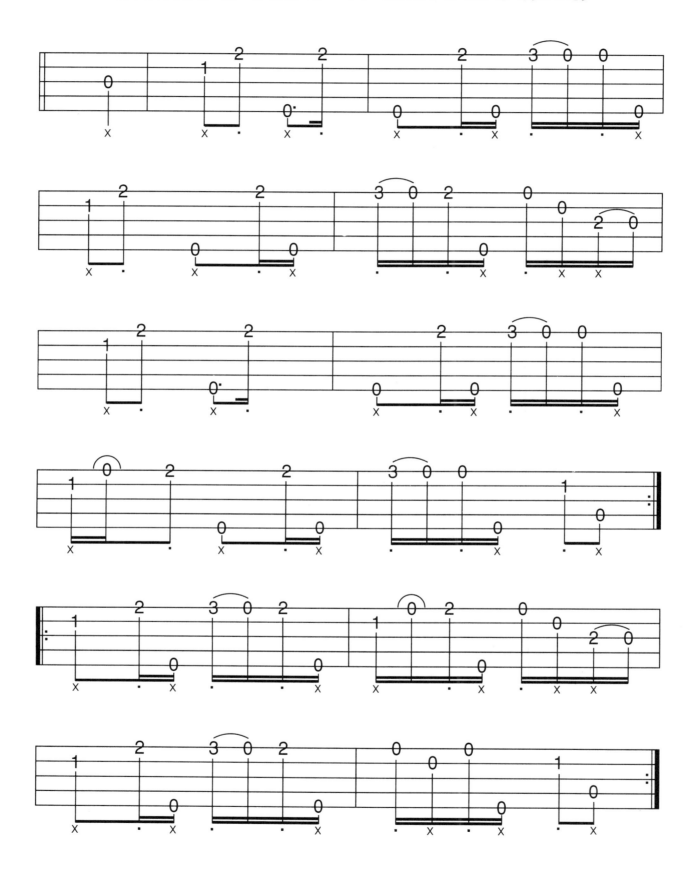

# Rumsey's Jig

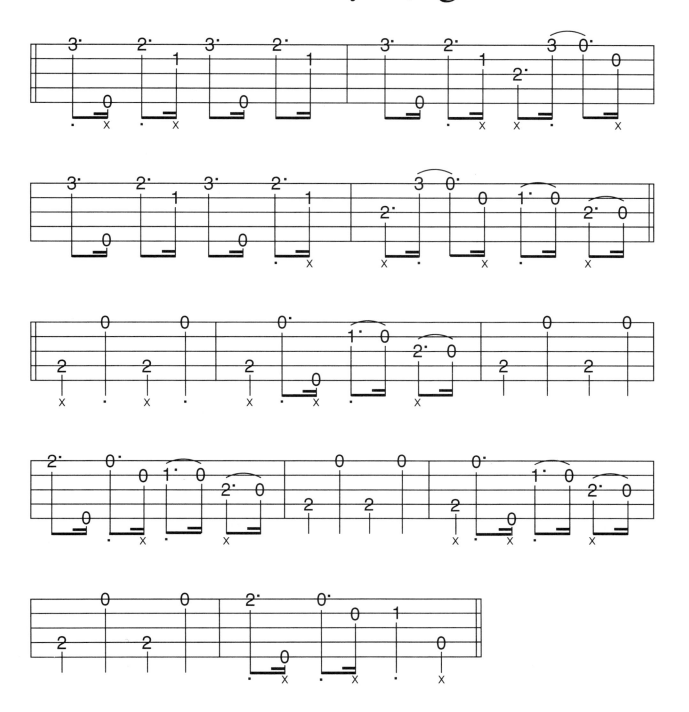

# Luke West's Walk Around

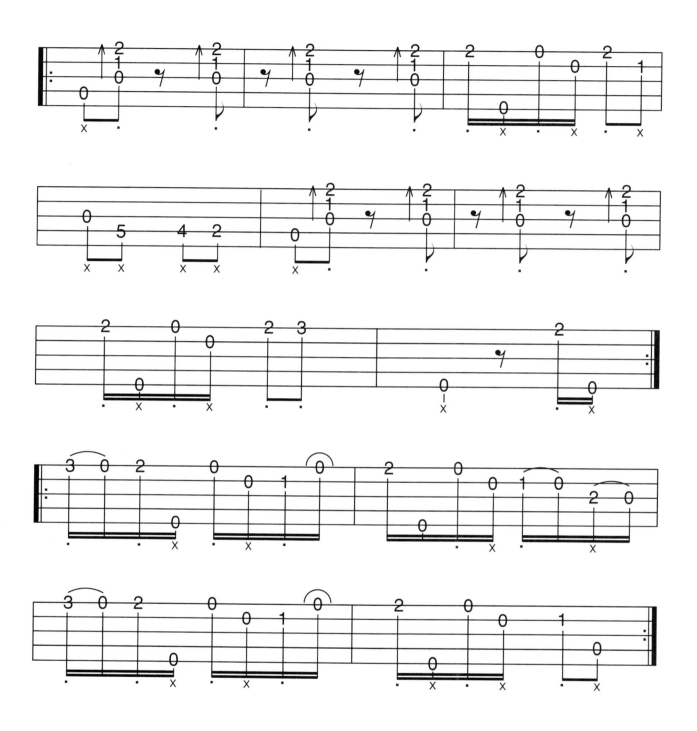

# Bully For You

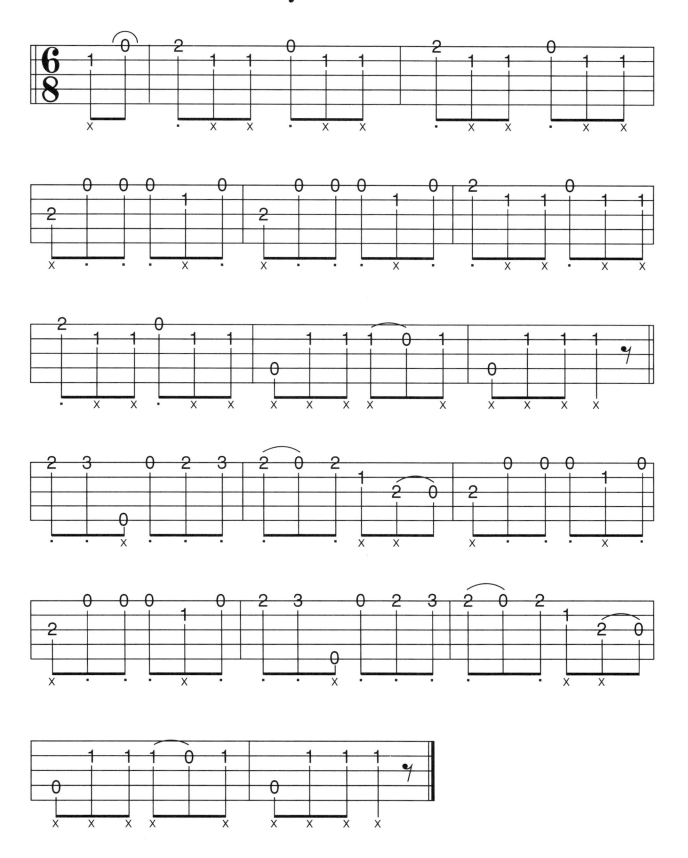

# Walk Into The Parlor

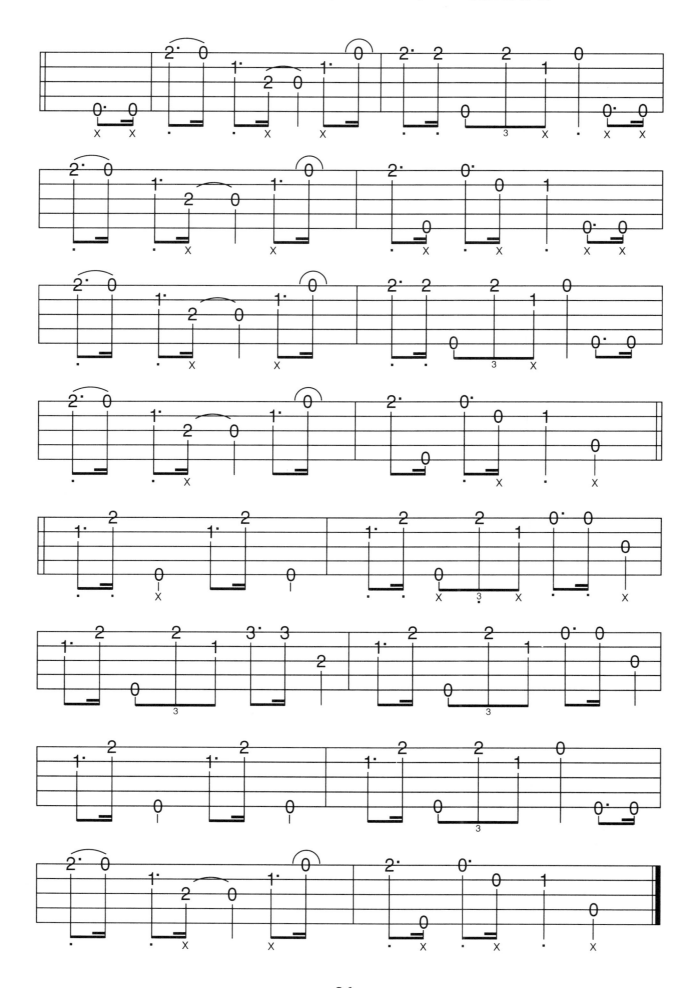

# Boston Jig

35

# Butler's Jig

# Hyde's Favorite

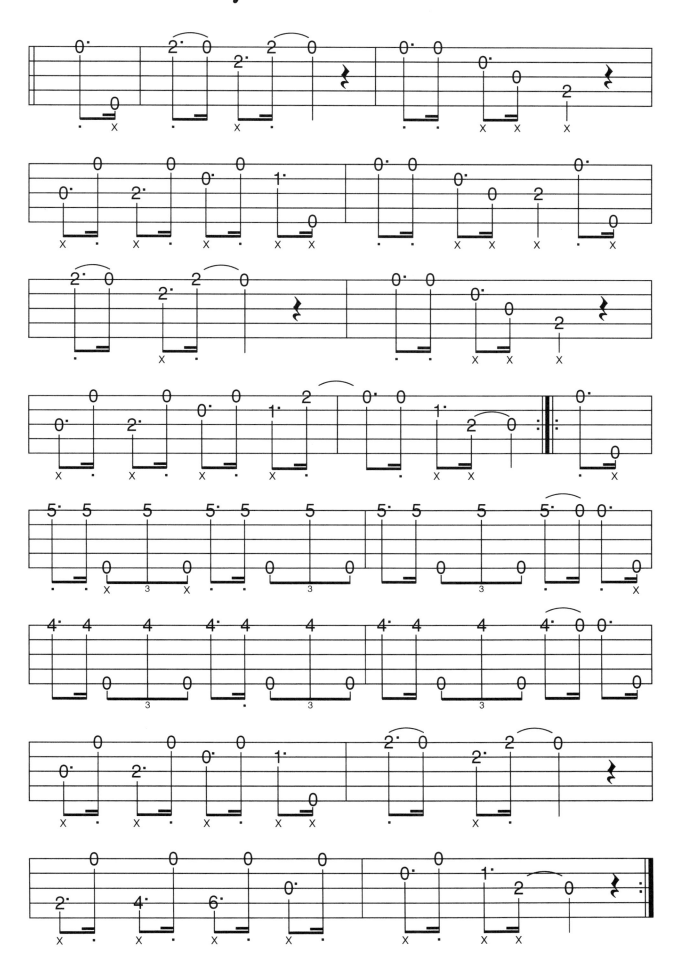

# Union Cockade

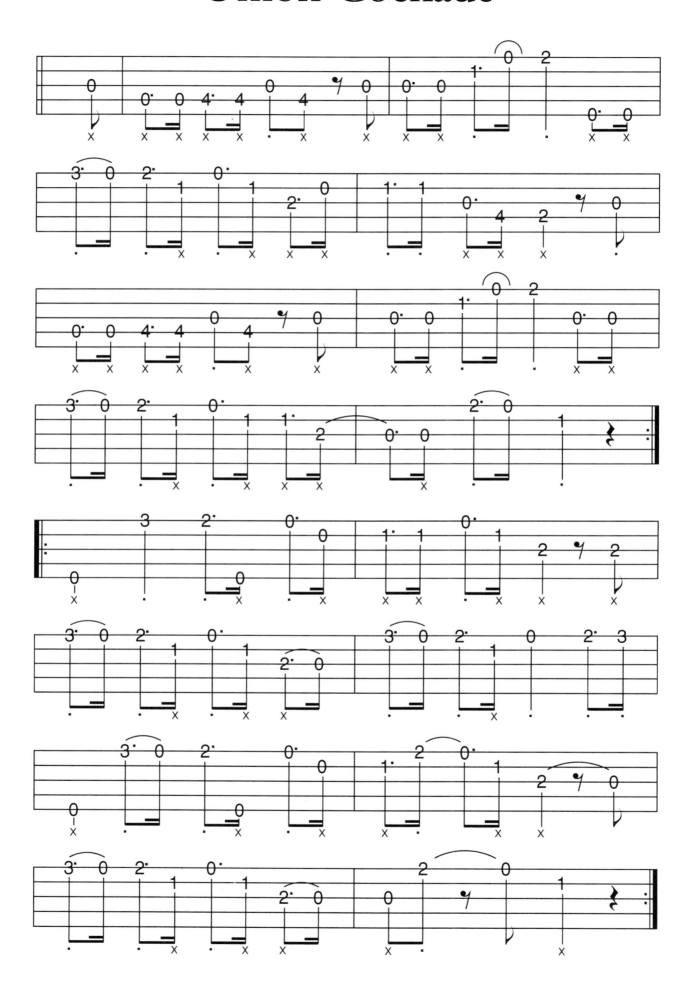

# Callowhill Jig

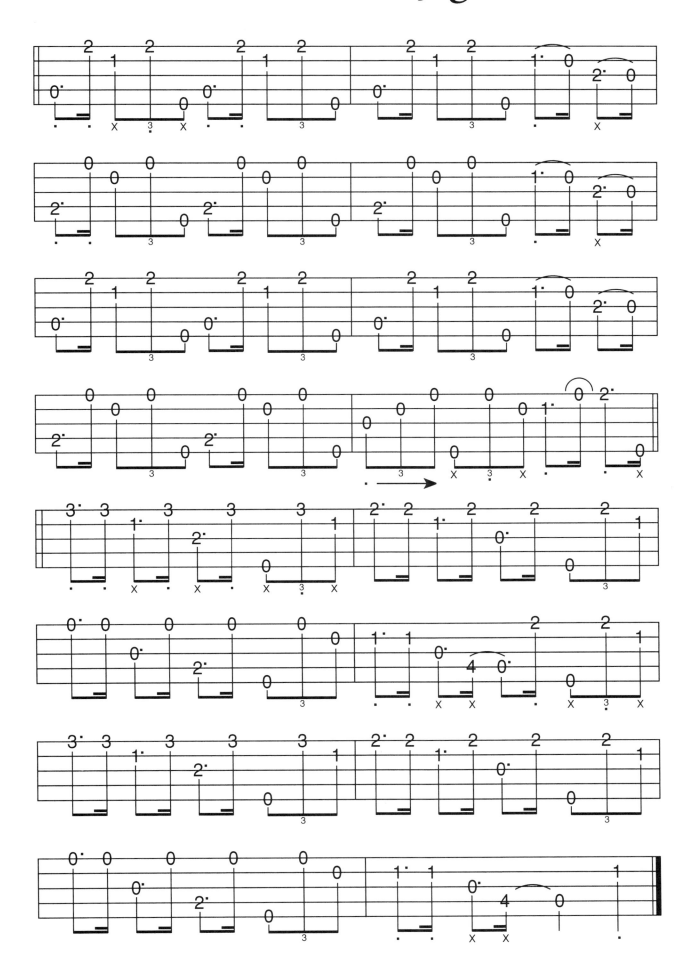

# My Love Is But A Lassie

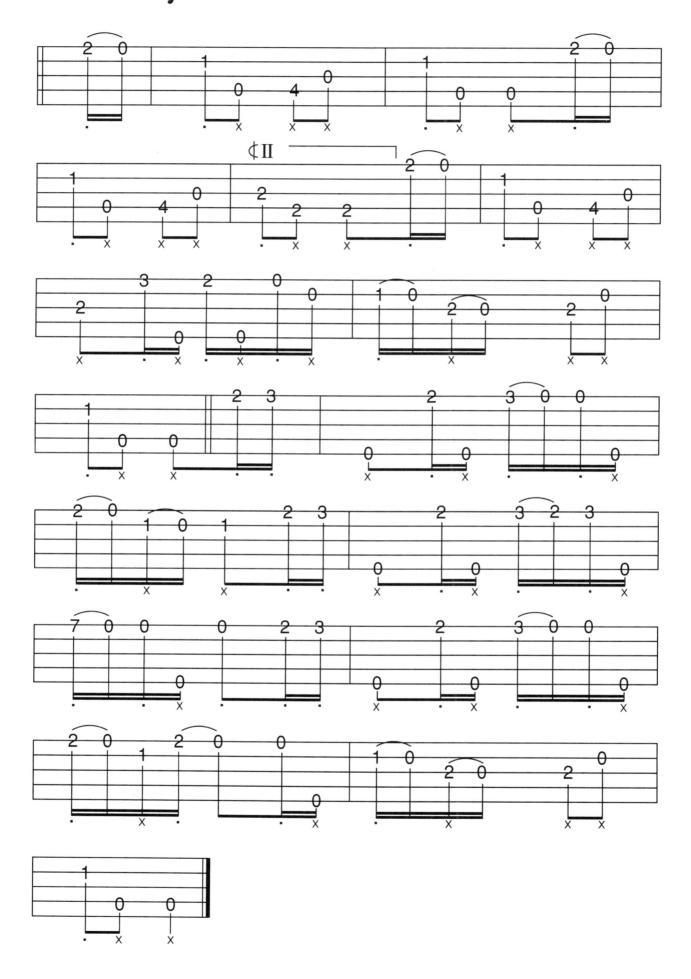

# Lanagan's Ball

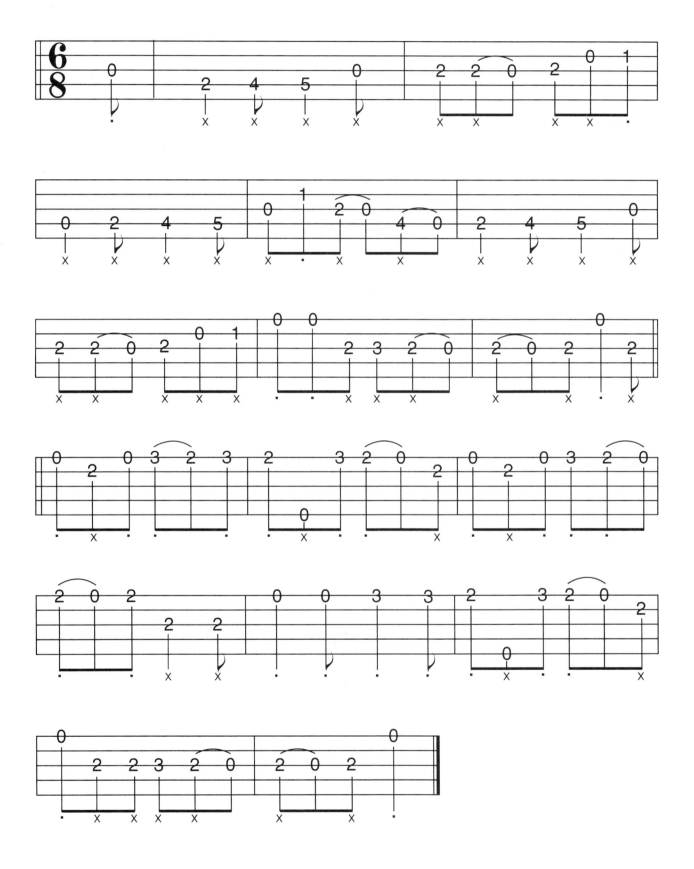

# O'Flarharty's Wake

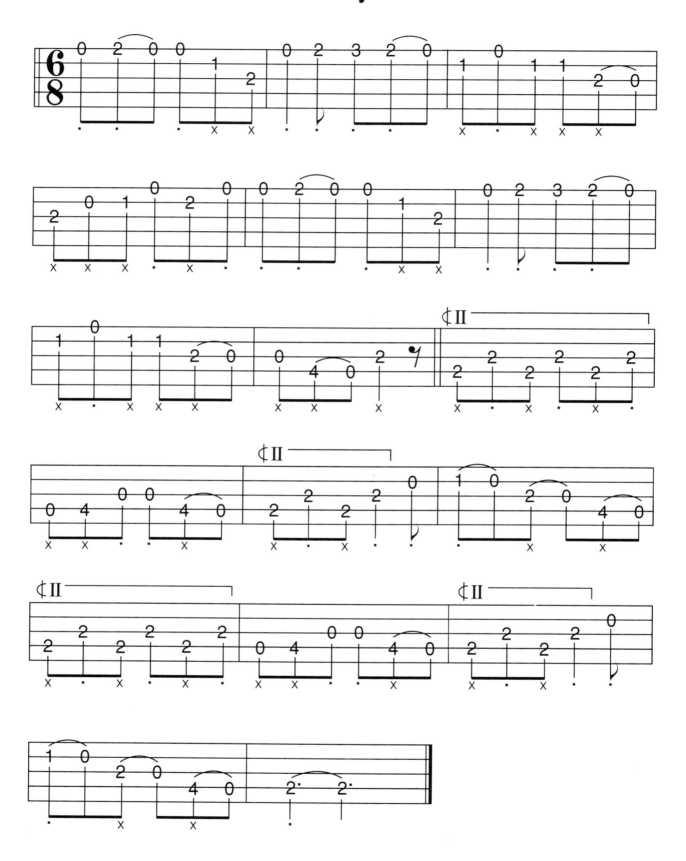

# Whole Hog Or None

# Charcoal Man (The)

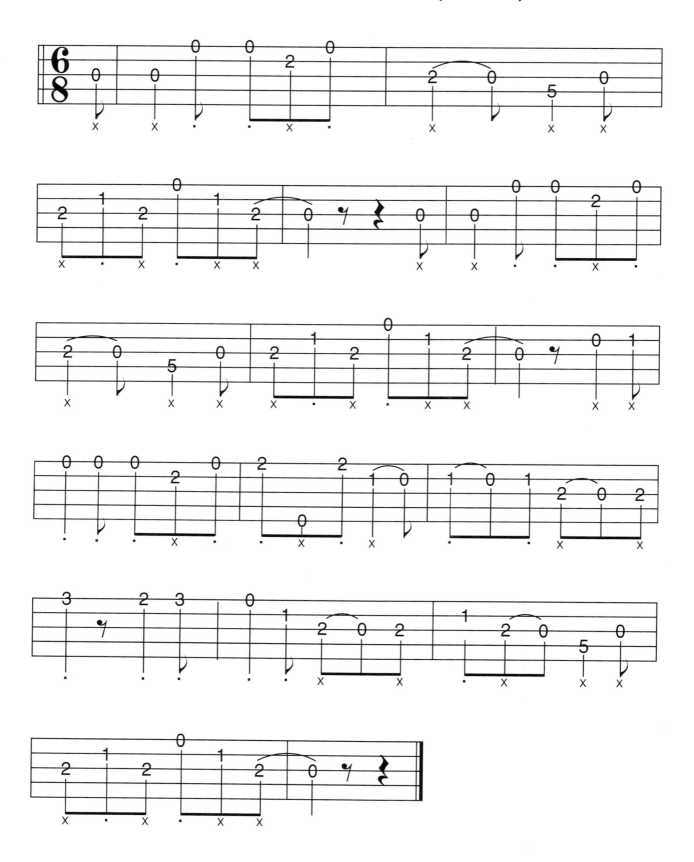

# Operatic Jig

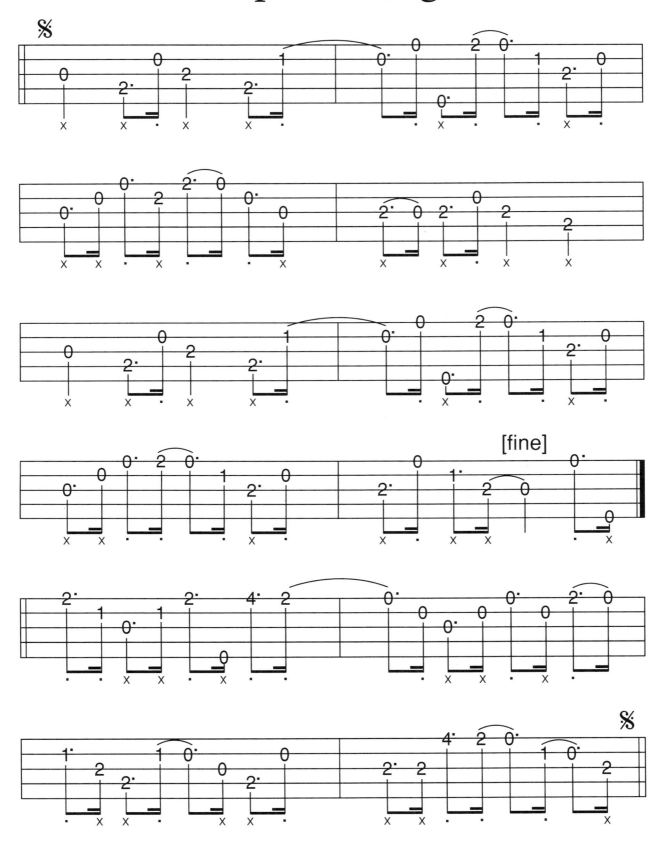

# Brighton Jig

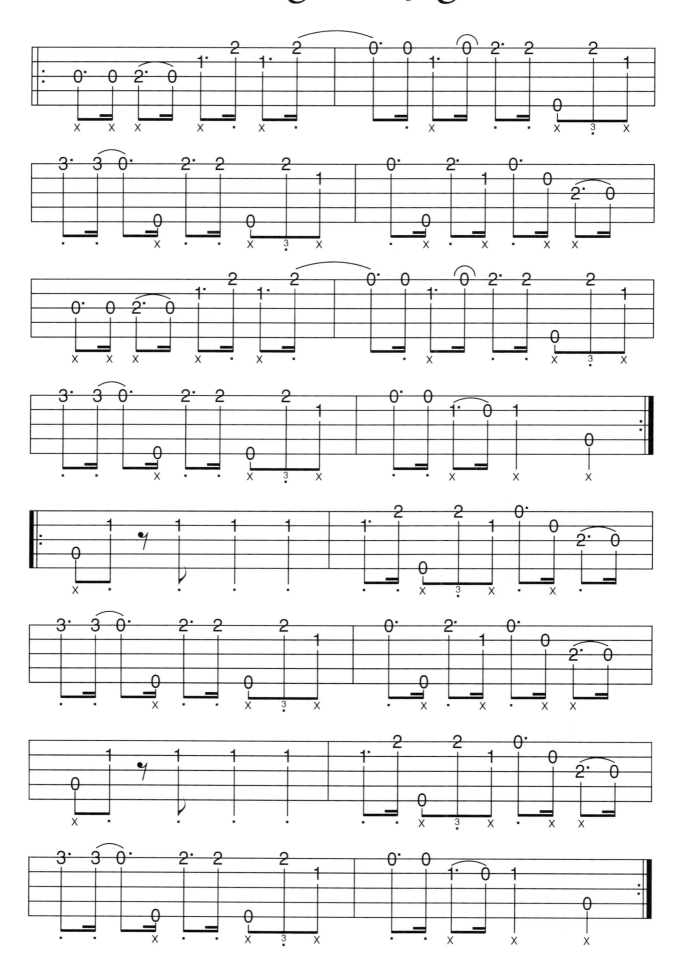

# Arkansas Traveler

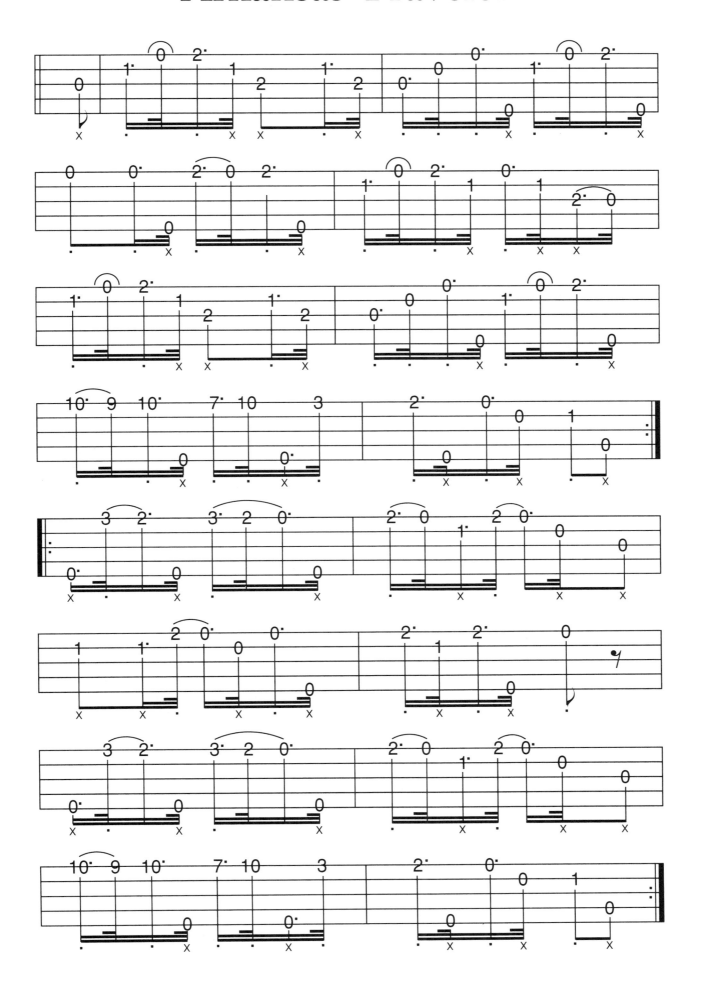

# Mike Ramsey
# Chanterelle Banjos

## Builders of Fine Open Back Banjos since 1985

Mike does custom work and specializes in 12" rims and in fretless banjos. He does mostly maple, cherry, walnut and mahogany banjos. Also engraving and carving. Color photos are available upon request. All banjos have a five year warranty, regardless of owner.

For a dealer near you write:

RR 2  Box 564-B
Appomattox, VA 24522

Call:  804 248-9615

On the Web:

http://members.aol.com/
banjoramse/banjo.htm